Xmas '0[...]

Dear Sunny & Greg Thompson,

We wish you a most happy holiday season.

It has been a pleasure having you stay with us.

Fondly—

Ruth & Elyn

Dreamers' Workshop

NEW HOPE PRESS

NEW HOPE, PA

THAT HOLY DREAM—
THAT HOLY DREAM,
WHILE ALL THE WORLD
WERE CHIDING,
HATH CHEERED
ME AS A LOVELY BEAM
A LONELY SPIRIT GUIDING.

EDGAR ALLEN POE

W ithin each of us there is another we do not know," wrote Swiss psychoanalyst Carl Jung. That someone, he added, speaks to us in dreams. Jung thought it possible that we dream continuously, though the din of consciousness often conceals this rich and fluid realm.

Many cultures have believed dreams to be visions from God. The ancient Egyptians created elaborate ceremonies to induce healing dreams. Joseph Campbell credited this inner wilderness as "the unquenchable source through which society is reborn." Many philosophers, scientists and artists have found great illumination in dreams, from Alexander the Great to Ingmar Bergman, who said, "All my pictures are dreams." Tom Edison napped purposefully through the day, always returning from dreamland with a new hypothesis. (Out of thousands he tried while developing the electric light, only a handful proved correct!) Friedrich Kekule found one of the building blocks of modern chemistry during a daydream in which he saw atoms literally dancing before his eyes.

A dream unrealized is like a life unlived, and thus what follows the enchantment of the dream is the dawning of the quest to see it realized. If you are following Thoreau's famous advice to "walk confidently in the direction of our dreams," *Dreamer's Workshop* offers a few words of encouragement for that heroic journey toward your heart's desire.

We are the music makers, we are the dreamers of dreams.

Arthur O'Shaughnessy

Harlequin, Raoul Dufy

Le Cirque, Georges Seurat

F THERE WERE DREAMS TO SELL, WHAT WOULD YOU BUY?

THOMAS LOVELL BEDDOES

Head of a Young Man, Albrecht Dürer

I'VE DREAMT
IN MY LIFE DREAMS THAT
HAVE STAYED WITH ME EVER
AFTER, AND CHANGED MY IDEAS;
THEY'VE GONE THROUGH AND
THROUGH ME, LIKE
WINE THROUGH WATER,
AND ALTERED THE COLOR
OF MY MIND.

EMILY BRONTE

Dreamer's Workshop

We are such stuff/ As dreams are made on,
and our little life/ Is rounded with a sleep.
Tempest

I have had a dream,
past the wit of man to say what dream it was.
A Midsummer Night's Dream

If I may trust the flattering
truth of sleep,/ My dreams presage
some joyful news at hand...
Romeo and Juliet

I profess not talking: only this,
Let each man do his best.
Henry IV

William Shakespeare

Things won are done, joy's soul lies in the doing.
Troilus and Cressida

They look into the beauty of thy mind,
And that, in guess, they measure by thy deeds.
Sonnet LXIX

Action is eloquence.
Coriolanus

Ambition should be made of sterner stuff.
Julius Caesar

From this moment,
The very firstlings of my heart shall be
The firstlings of my hand. And even now,
To crown my thoughts with acts, be it thought and done.
Macbeth

Our remedies oft in ourselves do lie;
Which we ascribe to heaven.
All's Well That Ends Well

Saskia and *Self portrait*,
Rembrandt

*I*MAGINATION
DISPOSES OF EVERYTHING;
IT CREATES BEAUTY,
JUSTICE AND HAPPINESS,
WHICH ARE EVERYTHING
IN THIS WORLD.

BLAISE PASCAL

If we dreamt the same thing every night, it would affect us as much
as the objects we see every day. And if a workman were sure to
dream every night for twelve hours' duration that he was a king,
I believe he would be almost as happy as a king, who should dream
every night for twelve hours on end that he was a workman.
Blaise Pascal

Imagination rules the world.
Napoleon Bonaparte

I maintain that ideas are events.
Gustave Flaubert

It seems to me that man is made to act rather than to know.
Frederick the Great

God did not call you to be canary-birds in a little cage, and
to hop up and down on three sticks, within a space no larger
than the size of the cage. God calls you to be eagles,
and to fly from sun to sun, over continents.
Henry Ward Beecher

I AM NOT
AFRAID OF
ANYTHING.
ELIZABETH I

Coronation portrait of Elizabeth I

THE GODS SELL US ALL GOOD THINGS FOR HARD WORK.

EPICHARMUS

Dost thou wish to rise? Begin by descending. You plan a tower that shall pierce the clouds? Lay first the foundations on humility.
St. Augustine

One must work, nothing but work. And one must have patience.
Auguste Rodin

What does God do all day? He/She gives birth.
Meister Eckhart

Do not wait for great strength before setting out...Do not wait to see very clearly before starting; one has to walk toward the light.
Philippe Vernier

There is suffering in the light; in excess it burns. Flame is hostile to the wing. To burn and yet to fly, this is the miracle of genius.
Victor Hugo

Think of ease, but work on.
George Herbert

St. Anthony, Albrecht Dürer

Dreamers Workshop

YOU WORK
THAT YOU MAY
KEEP PEACE
WITH THE
EARTH AND
THE SOUL OF
THE EARTH.

KAHLIL GIBRAN

Spring, Peter Bruegel the Elder

*I*T IS
MY FIRM
CONVICTION
THAT ALL
GOOD ACTION
IS BOUND TO
BEAR FRUIT
IN THE END.

MAHATMA GANDHI

Drawing, Charles Percier

*D*ARE AND
THE WORLD ALWAYS
YIELDS; OR IF IT BEATS
YOU SOMETIMES, DARE
IT AGAIN AND IT
WILL SUCCUMB.
WILLIAM MAKEPEACE THACKERAY

Of course, out of every hundred
adventures you embark on, ninety-nine
don't work out the way you hoped. I've been
blanket-tossed and I've been bruised; still, nothing
can compare with waiting for the next adventure.
Miguel Cervantes

All things are possible until they are proved
impossible—even the impossible
may only be so as of now.
Pearl S. Buck

Either I will find a way, or I will make one.
Philip Sidney

This thing that we call failure is not the
falling down, but the staying down.
Mary Pickford

Risk! Risk anything! ...Do the hardest thing on earth
for you. Act for yourself.
Katherine Mansfield

Dreamers' Workshop

DOUBT IS A PAIN
TOO LONELY TO KNOW
THAT FAITH IS HIS
TWIN BROTHER.

KAHLIL GIBRAN

WE MUST WALK CONSCIOUSLY ONLY PART WAY TOWARD OUR GOAL, AND THEN LEAP IN THE DARK TO OUR SUCCESS.

HENRY DAVID THOREAU

Sketches, Edgar Degas

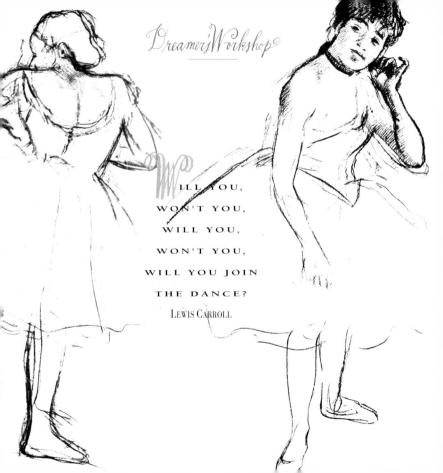

Dreamer's Workshop

WILL YOU,
WON'T YOU,
WILL YOU,
WON'T YOU,
WILL YOU JOIN
THE DANCE?

LEWIS CARROLL

Dreamers Workshop

Our tragedy today is a general and universal physical fear so long sustained by now that we can even bear it...Because of this, the young man or woman writing today has forgotten the problems of the human heart in conflict with itself which alone can make good writing because only that is worth writing about, worth the agony and the sweat.

He must learn them again. He must teach himself that the basest of all things is to be afraid: and, teaching himself that, forget it forever, leaving no room in his workshop for anything but the old verities and truths of the heart, the universal truths lacking which any story is ephemeral and doomed—love and honor and pity and pride and compassion and sacrifice.

WILLIAM FAULKNER

Charlie Chaplin in *Sunnyside*, 1919.

$\mathcal{F}$AILURE IS UNIMPORTANT.

IT TAKES COURAGE TO

MAKE A FOOL OF YOURSELF.

CHARLIE CHAPLIN

Do it if you're going to do it.
Plautus

Do what you can, with what you have, where you are.
Teddy Roosevelt

Doing is the great thing.
John Ruskin

Do not wait for leaders; do it
alone, person to person.
Mother Teresa

Scorn trifles, lift your aims; do what you are afraid to do.
Mary Moody Emerson

Do the thing and you have still the power; but
they who do not the thing have not the power.
Ralph Waldo Emerson

The dog that trots about finds a bone.
Gypsy Proverb

All things are just as you make them.
Plautus

It is never too late to be what you might have been.
George Eliot

God's gifts put man's best dreams
to shame.
Elizabeth Barrett Browning

The most pathetic person in the world is
someone who has sight, but has no vision.
Helen Keller

Now, at the time of the fabulous artificer, he seemed
to hear the noise of dim waves and to see a winged
form flying above the waves and slowly climbing the
air...a symbol of the artist forging anew and in his
workshop out of the sluggish matter of the earth a
new soaring impalpable imperishable being?
James Joyce

The Astronomer, Engraving after Vermeer

$\mathcal{I}$ HAVE GOT A
FEW WONDERFUL IDEAS
IN MY HEAD WHICH
HAVE TO BE WORKED
OUT IN DUE COURSE.

ALBERT EINSTEIN

Dreamer's Workshop

The most beautiful emotion we can experience is the mystical.
It is the source of all true art and science.
Albert Einstein

Too low they build who build beneath the stars.
Edward Young

Raise thy head; take stars for money.
George Herbert

Uncharted orbits call me, new dominions
of sheer creation, active without end.
This higher life, joys that no mortal won!
Upon the mild light of the earthly sun
Turn bold, your back! And with undaunted daring
Tear open the eternal portals
Past which all creatures slink in silent dread.
The time has come to prove by deeds that mortals
Have as much dignity as any god.
Goethe

Drawing, Flaminio Innocenzo Minozzi

I admire the skill which, on the sea-shore, makes the tides
drive wheels and grind corn, and which thus engages the
assistance of the moon, like a hired hand. Now that is the wisdom
of a man, in every instance of his labor, to hitch his wagon
to a star, and see his chore done by the gods themselves.
Ralph Waldo Emerson

The universe is full of magical things patiently waiting
for our wits to grow sharper.
Eden Phillpotts

The self shines in space through knowing.
The Upanishads

The dream is the small hidden door in the deepest and most intimate
sanctum of the soul, which opens into the primeval cosmic night.
Carl Jung

We are all in the gutter,
but some of us are looking at the stars.
Oscar Wilde

YOU'LL BE BOTHERED FROM TIME TO TIME BY STORMS, FOG, SNOW. WHEN YOU ARE, THINK OF THOSE WHO WENT THROUGH IT BEFORE YOU, AND SAY TO YOURSELF, "WHAT THEY COULD DO, I CAN DO."

ANTOINE DE SAINT-EXUPÉRY

Dreamers Workshop

COURAGE IS THE
PRICE THAT LIFE EXTRACTS
FOR GRANTING PEACE.
THE SOUL THAT KNOWS IT
NOT, KNOWS NO RELEASE
FROM LITTLE THINGS;
KNOWS NOT THE LIVID
LONELINESS OF FEAR, NOR
MOUNTAIN HEIGHTS WHERE
BETTER JOY CAN HEAR THE
SOUND OF WINGS.

AMELIA EARHART

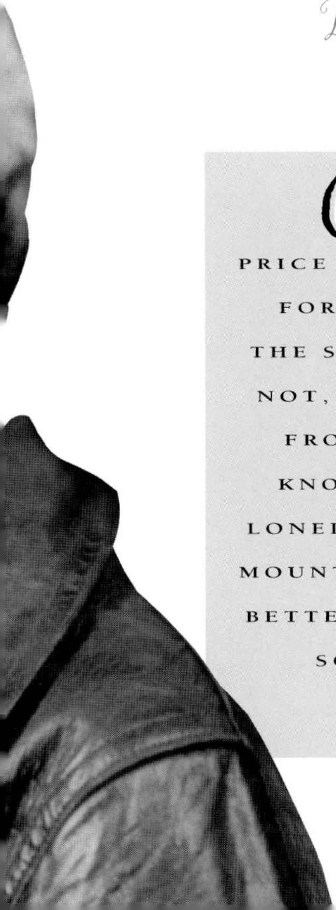

Amelia Earhart

Dreamer's Workshop

Angel, Marc Chagall

A rock pile ceases to be a rock pile the moment a single man contemplates it, bearing within him the image of a cathedral...What I do see more clearly now is the prime agent of victory. He who bears in his heart a cathedral to be built is already victorious...Victory is the fruit of love. Only love can say what face shall emerge from the clay. Only love can guide man towards that face. Intelligence is valid only as it serves love.

The sculptor is great with the burden of his creation. It matters little that he know not how he will draw it forth from the clay. From one thumb stroke to the next, from error to error, contradiction to contradiction, he will move through the clay towards his creation.

ANTOINE DE SAINT-EXUPÉRY

Dreamer's Workshop

KEEP ADDING,
KEEP WALKING,
KEEP ADVANCING;
DO NOT STOP,
DO NOT TURN BACK,
DO NOT TURN FROM
THE STRAIGHT ROAD.

ST. AUGUSTINE

Avenue of Poplars, Vincent van Gogh

Dreamer's Workshop

All great ideas, the races' aspirations, all heroisms,
deeds of rapt enthusiasts, be ye my Gods.
Walt Whitman

Even in our own dulled and clouded hearts,
when the radiance of God beats upon them, we see
sometimes an answering gleam within, like the
secret fire that sleeps in the uncut gem.
Arthur Christopher Benson

Better with naked nerve to bear/The needles of this
goading air,/Than in the lap of sensual ease, forego/
The godlike power to do, the godlike aim to know.
John Greenleaf Whittier

And all that you are sorry for is what
you haven't done.
Margaret Widdemer

I would give all the wealth of the world, and all the
deeds of the heroes, for one true vision.
Henry David Thoreau

I have heard talk and talk. Good words do not last long until they amount to something.
Chief Joseph

Don't make excuses. Make good.
Elbert Hubbard

Remember that it is not enough to have the method, and the art, and the power, nor even that which is touch, but you shall have also the conviction that nails the work to the wall.
Rudyard Kipling

Will...is the foundation of all being; it is part and parcel of every creature, and the permanent element in everything.
Arthur Schopenhauer

Invention, it must be humbly admitted, does not consist of creating out of voice, but out of chaos.
Mary Shelley

> ONLY AN
> INVENTOR KNOWS
> HOW TO BORROW,
> AND EVERY MAN IS
> OR SHOULD BE
> AN INVENTOR.
>
> RALPH WALDO EMERSON

Illustration, Maxfield Parrish

Dreamer's Workshop

STICKING TO IT IS THE GENIUS! ANY OTHER BRIGHT-MINDED FELLOW CAN ACCOMPLISH JUST AS MUCH IF HE WILL STICK LIKE HELL AND REMEMBER NOTHING THAT'S ANY GOOD WORKS BY ITSELF. YOU GOT TO MAKE THE DAMN THING WORK.

THOMAS EDISON

I'LL NEVER GIVE UP, FOR I MAY HAVE A STREAK OF LUCK BEFORE I DIE.

THOMAS EDISON

Thomas Edison, John Burroughs, Henry Ford and Harvey Firestone

I WANT NONE OF THE RICH MAN'S
USUAL TOYS. I WANT NO HORSES
OR YACHTS...WHAT I WANT IS
A PERFECT WORKSHOP.

THOMAS EDISON

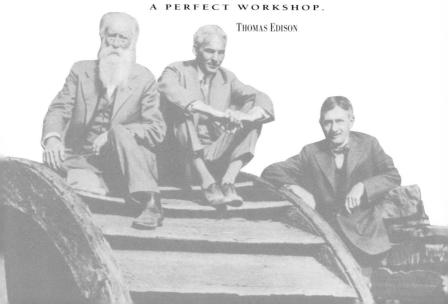

GREAT MINDS HAVE PURPOSES, OTHERS HAVE WISHES.

WASHINGTON IRVING

St. Jerome Beside A Pollard Willow, Rembrandt